W9-BEW-087

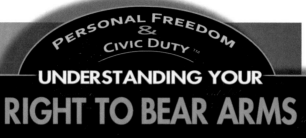

PERSONAL FREEDOM & CIVIC DUTY ™

UNDERSTANDING YOUR
RIGHT TO BEAR ARMS

Nathaniel Cross and
Michael A. Sommers

ROSEN
PUBLISHING®

New York

Published in 2012 by The Rosen Publishing Group, Inc.
29 East 21st Street, New York, NY 10010

First Edition

Library of Congress Cataloging-in-Publication Data

Cross, Nathaniel, 1978–
Understanding your right to bear arms/Nathaniel Cross, Michael A. Sommers.
    p. cm.—(Personal freedom and civic duty)
Includes bibliographical references and index.
ISBN 978-1-4488-4664-1 (library binding)
1. Firearms—Law and legislation—United States. 2. Gun control—United States. 3. United States. Constitution. 2nd Amendment. I. Sommers, Michael A., 1966– II. Title.
KF3941.C76 2011
344.7305'33—dc22
                                                    2010048423

Manufactured in the United States of America

CPSIA Compliance Information: Batch #S11YA: For further information, contact Rosen Publishing, New York, New York, at 1-800-237-9932.

On the cover: Gun rights activists take part in a Second Amendment march on April 19, 2010, in Washington, D.C.

CONTENTS

INTRODUCTION

I n 2010, according to the National Rifle Association (NRA) Institute for Legislative Action, there were roughly three hundred million firearms owned by civilians in the United States. This calculates to roughly one firearm per person in America. According to a 2005 survey by Gallup, 67 percent of gun owners said they own firearms for protection against crime. According to the Federal Bureau of Investigation (FBI), roughly 16,272 murders were committed

Above: The right to bear arms has been a highly debated issue for many years. Supporters of gun rights argue that firearms are necessary for the protection of citizens from criminals.

in the United States during 2008. Of these, about 10,886 or 67 percent were committed with firearms. According to the Centers for Disease Control and Prevention (CDC), guns are responsible for more than 38,000 deaths each year in the United States.

These statistics illustrate debate over gun control. While those who are for gun control argue that firearms are a tool of criminals, those who are for the right to bear arms claim that firearms are necessary to combat crime. These shocking numbers have also triggered a lot of debate about guns. Some people think that guns are a problem and that there should be stricter laws that make it more difficult to own, carry, or use such weapons. Some people even believe that guns should be banned altogether. On the other side of the debate are those who think that the responsibility for these violent acts lies not with guns, but with the individuals who use them. Such people believe that Americans have the right to protect themselves, their loved ones, and their property—they have the right to "keep and bear arms."

This idea—the right of the people to keep and bear arms—is not just a slogan. It is the central part of the Second Amendment of the U.S. Constitution. The Second Amendment states: "A well regulated Militia, being necessary to the security of a free State, the right of the people to keep and bear Arms, shall not be infringed." These words were written by the drafters of the Constitution more than two hundred years ago. One of the ten original amendments that make up the Bill of Rights, the right to bear arms has long been seen as one of the fundamental liberties of every American citizen. But in the last two centuries, America has changed a lot. So have both Americans, and the "arms" they use. Has this changed the way America's politicians, courts of justice, and citizens view this basic American right?

THE SECOND AMENDMENT TODAY

We are now in the second decade of the new millennium, and the role of guns in our society has never been as hotly debated as it is today. At the same time, guns seem to be everywhere. They are featured in popular movies and on prime-time TV shows. They are all over the news.

An independent survey found that 66 percent of Americans think gun control is more important than the rights of gun owners (29 percent think the opposite). Yet many of these same Americans, like members of the NRA and other gun control opponents, doubt that tighter restrictions will solve the problem of gun-related violence in this country. Many believe community programs for young people and tougher prison terms would be much more effective than tougher gun laws. Only 6 percent of those surveyed thought stricter gun laws could have prevented a tragedy like the Columbine massacre.

GUN LAWS WORLDWIDE

Much of the rest of the world thinks that America is a violent place. In almost no other part of the world are private citizens as free to own and use guns as in the United States. The mass production of guns and their constant presence on television, in films, and in the press has made them a big part of American life. So has the Second Amendment.

The United States is the only developed nation in which guns are such a big part of the culture. With more than three hundred million firearms in the United States as of 2010, there is roughly one gun for every man, woman, and child in the country. These are very high numbers for a nation with secure borders, a nuclear defense system, and armed police. Citizens who are allowed to own guns must go through waiting periods, register their arms, and have licenses to use them. Gun control advocates point to other countries and their tight gun laws as model examples of what could happen in the United States if more restrictions were placed on guns. Yet aside from the fact that it is much more difficult to simply get a gun in these countries, there is also an important cultural factor involved. Many citizens of these other countries quite simply don't want or don't feel they need a gun. Guns are not—and never have been—part of their culture.

An interesting exception is the case of Switzerland. In this tiny European country, a larger percentage of private citizens own guns than in the United States This is because instead of relying on a permanent

Since the United States was founded on rebellion against government by its citizens, its gun laws have always been well protected. With the right security clearances, guns can be bought almost anywhere.

army, Switzerland depends on a militia of armed citizens for defense. As a result, almost every adult male is legally obliged to own a gun. The Swiss government actually supplies enlisted men with automatic assault weapons and pistols. At the same time, Switzerland has one of the lowest gun-related murder rates of any industrialized nation. Gun control opponents say this proves that the problem in America isn't guns themselves; it's the people who use, or misuse, them.

This raises some complicated questions. Why is there so much violence in America today? Is it because

INTERPRETATION OF THE SECOND AMENDMENT

There have been a few cases that interpret the Bill of Rights a certain way. These rulings affected further federal and local rulings and regulations.

1857—*Dred Scott v. Sandford*
Dred Scott, a black man, was denied the rights of all citizens, including the right to bear arms, based on his race. At the time, slaves were not acknowledged as free men or true citizens. This decision was interpreted to mean that free men did have the right to bear arms, regardless if in a militia. The right to bear arms was interpreted as equal to the right to free speech, as long as you were recognized as a U.S. citizen.

1939—*United States v. Miller*
Jack Miller was a bank robber who drove across state lines with a customized shotgun. The court found that the Second Amendment did not protect citizens who used weapons that were not part of standard militia use. This was interpreted to mean that a person could have guns, but the Second Amendment did not guarantee a person's right to have any kind of gun without collective approval and regulation.

of the presence of so many guns? Or is it people's attitudes in relation to guns? Are there just too many violent individuals in the United States? Or is our society as a whole violent? Maybe a combination of these factors is to blame. Or perhaps the blame lies somewhere else altogether.

HOW PEOPLE VIEW THE SECOND AMENDMENT

The right to bear arms is a very serious and complicated issue. After all, guns are quite literally a matter of life and death. And the United States has a very serious gun problem, with rates of gun-related murders, accidents, suicides, and violence far outnumbering those of other industrialized nations. At the same time, the right to bear arms is part of American culture and history. It is a fundamental right that guarantees citizens the right to protect themselves, their homes, and their loved ones.

What is the solution? Is it placing even more restrictions on guns? Is it banning them altogether? Is it requiring that young people learn about gun safety and how to shoot accurately? These questions are difficult to answer. However, as America steps into the twenty-first century, more and more people are trying. Although many voices are speaking out and being heard, almost all can be divided into one of two camps.

There are those who believe that the right to bear arms is an absolute right of each and every American citizen. These people are known as gun control opponents. They see every bill or law that places restrictions on gun ownership or use as an infringement of their fundamental American rights guaranteed under the Second Amendment.

Gun rights activists cheer after a 5–4 Supreme Court ruling on June 26, 2008, that banning guns in Washington, D.C., violates the Second Amendment.

Then there are those who believe that America has changed significantly since the Founding Fathers drafted the Constitution. They believe that the common safety and security of everybody is more important than the nonessential right of an individual. They believe that gun-related violence in the United States is out of hand. And the only way to control it is to create laws that limit or even ban ownership and use of guns.

Both those who support and those who oppose gun control have interesting, logical, and valid arguments. They use these arguments to make Americans aware of the role of guns in society. They also use them to lobby lawmakers of both state and federal governments. Lobbying is an organized attempt to influence lawmakers to vote for or against a specific law. As you discover both opponents' and supporters' points of view, think hard about where you and the people you know stand on gun control.

ARGUMENTS AGAINST GUN CONTROL

The Second Amendment of the U.S. Constitution—the "law of the land"—gives each American citizen "the right to keep and bear arms."

- The majority of state constitutions give individual citizens the right to bear arms.
- Police can't be everywhere at once. By the time they arrive at the scene of a crime, the damage has already been done.
- Protecting oneself and one's family and property is the right and duty of every American citizen.
- Criminals are afraid of guns. Statistics show that they are less likely to attack, assault, rape, rob, or break into the house of somebody if they suspect or know that person owns a gun.
- According to a 2005 Gallup poll, gun control affects the 41 percent of gun owners who like to

GUN RIGHTS TODAY

Currently, as of 2011, Americans have the right to keep and bear arms without being part of a militia. While you may have this right, you must follow government regulations. In most states, you must obtain permits to purchase and carry a gun. You cannot have a permit without a background check to make sure that you are a responsible citizen. These are known as Brady background checks.

Permits are granted by state and local governments, not the federal government. This means that each state has its own permit laws. For instance, Virginia and Alaska do not require a person to have a permit in order to purchase handguns and long guns.

There are regulations set forth by the federal government that are generally followed by most states. Typically, you cannot obtain a gun permit if you:

- Have been convicted or found guilty of a crime for which you served more than one year of prison time.
- Have been convicted or found guilty of domestic violence.
- Are a fugitive or escapee from justice.
- Are a user of any illegal drug.
- Have a history of mental illness or have been committed to a mental institution.
- Are not a legal U.S. citizen or a legally cleared immigrant.
- Have been released from military service under dishonorable conditions.
- Have a restraining order filed against you. A restraining order is a court order to keep away from someone who believes you are stalking, threatening, or harassing him or her.

According to federal firearms regulations, it is illegal for a person under the age of eighteen to have a gun. A parent may purchase a gun for a minor but only for limited uses. These uses include ranching, farming, and hunting.

A legal gun is one that is made by a licensed manufacturer. The guns are sent to a licensed gun store, where they can be purchased by a legally cleared person. Again, some states may not require a permit for purchase, but the gun must be legally distributed nonetheless. Any other way of obtaining a gun is illegal. If you know of a gun that was not obtained legally, discreetly tell your parent, guardian, or teacher about it. That gun may have a history that could get its current owner into a lot of trouble.

hunt for recreation. Hunters claim that registration and licensing fees that gun control laws impose on them make this traditional American sport unaffordable for many people.

- Gun control has done nothing to reduce crime. Opponents point to many situations in which states or cities passed laws restricting the purchase or possession of certain types of firearms only to find that gun-related crimes increased. They feel the solution is not restricting guns (which only hurts law-abiding citizens, as criminals can always buy a gun illegally off the street), but toughening crime laws and increasing prison terms for convicted criminals.

ORGANIZATIONS AGAINST GUN CONTROL

There are quite a few organizations that oppose gun control and support the right of private citizens to own and use guns. Some of the best known include the Second Amendment Foundation and the Citizens Committee for the Right to Keep and Bear Arms. Of course, the biggest, most organized, and most influential of these organizations is the NRA.

The NRA fiercely defends individuals' rights to bear arms, and it organizes a great many public awareness campaigns to convince people that the violence in America is not caused by guns, but by people. Well-organized and with a large budget, the organization fiercely fights any attempt at creating new gun control laws. It sees each new law as a further restriction of a fundamental American right. The NRA's position is summed up in its famous slogan: "Guns don't kill, people do."

The NRA says the problem is not guns themselves but people who don't know how to use them. To try and fix this, the NRA has developed gun safety and awareness programs in communities throughout the

The National Rifle Association, which advocates for gun rights, is such a powerful force that politicians regularly campaign to its numerous members in hopes of securing their votes.

United States. And for over two decades, it has run a gun safety campaign aimed specifically at kids. The Eddie Eagle GunSafe Program features a cartoon eagle named Eddie who lets kids know that guns aren't toys. Eddie gives safety tips and teaches kids what to do if they come across a gun (get away from it and then tell an adult).

SUPPORTERS OF GUN CONTROL

Congressional hearings have featured testimony by many witnesses who tell stories about how having a gun saved their lives and/or the lives of others. Most of these stories are very convincing. However, these stories are often selected to reinforce a point of view. Equally convincing stories can be told about people who are killed or seriously injured when they pull out their guns and try to defend themselves.

There are many stories about people who bought guns to protect themselves and their homes and wound up killing themselves or others because they didn't know how to handle a gun. And although the NRA teaches courses in gun safety, it opposes any law that would make such training obligatory before obtaining a license to buy a gun. Many people who try to defend themselves with guns become gun victims themselves. Worse, hardly a week goes by without a news story about a child who was shot, hurt, or killed by a gun kept in the home in the honest belief that it was there for protection.

People who support gun control feel that the gun situation has gotten out of control in the United States. The number of shootings in schools, homes, and offices across the country has mobilized many people who feel something needs to be done. Their solution is more gun control. Gun control can mean many things. It can mean requiring people who buy guns to register them so that the guns can be traced.

Arguments for Gun Control

According to the U.S. Census Bureau in 2005, people aged seventeen through nineteen were 4.3 percent of

Opponents of gun rights protest against the Supreme Court's 5–4 ruling on June 26, 2008, allowing firearms to be carried in Washington, D.C.

the overall population of the United States but accounted for 11.2 percent of those killed by firearm homicides.

The Second Amendment does not give individual citizens the absolute right to keep and bear arms.

Throughout American history, state courts, federal courts, and the Supreme Court have ruled that both federal and state governments have the right to limit the private ownership and use of guns.

The United States is not the same place it was more than two centuries ago when guns were necessary for colonists' survival (hunting food, protection from hostile Indians, and self-protection in the absence of police). Gun-related violence and deaths are a major social problem that just keeps getting worse. Other industrialized nations with strict gun control laws have far fewer murders, suicides, and gun-related deaths and injuries.

Gun control can mean having a waiting period, which allows police to do a background check on the purchaser. It can mean having a license to own and carry a gun. It can mean prohibiting or limiting the sale, ownership, or possession of certain types of firearms in certain places or prohibiting certain people from owning guns. It can mean obliging gun owners to store their arms safely. It can mean putting safety locks on guns and triggers for which only owners have the key or combination.

Gun control supporters feel that the federal government is the only authority with the power to control the arms industries and people's access to guns. Few believe that guns should be banned completely. But they do feel that too many guns are ending up too easily in the wrong hands.

Most gun control advocates respect the Second Amendment. However, they tend to have a different interpretation of this controversial amendment. Many don't believe that it gives individual citizens the absolute right to keep and bear arms. Instead they see the amendment as a collective right of a state's militia to bear arms in order to defend themselves. A staunch supporter of this view is former Supreme Court Chief Justice Warren Burger who once argued: "Is there any question that a citizen has the right to own and keep an automobile? Yet we accept the state's power to regulate its purchase and to license the vehicle and its driver. Should guns be any different?"

THE RIGHT TO BEAR ARMS:
A HISTORY

CHAPTER 2

Today there is no other nation in the Western world in which bearing arms is such a treasured, and hotly debated, constitutional "right." These days, both Americans and citizens around the world talk of the United States' unique "gun culture." It is impossible to imagine guns not being part of U.S. culture. After all, recent statistics show that there are currently enough arms in America to outfit every man, woman, and child. But guns are not only an important part of the country's present; they also constitute an important part of the past. Guns have played a significant role in America's very unique history. The use of and attitude toward them have, for better or for worse, shaped who Americans are as a people and as a nation.

In order to understand who Americans are today, it is essential to look at the past. More specifically, we need to look at the special group of individuals who created this country after the first thirteen states of the United States of America went to war and won their independence from England. Known as the Founding Fathers, they were the ones who wrote the

22

country's Constitution and Bill of Rights—documents that mapped out how this new and democratic nation would be governed.

In fact, the Constitution and Bill of Rights went beyond simply making up the rules that would govern American citizens. They defined what America would be and what it would become. Since part of that definition included the right to bear arms, we need to look at why arms were so important and what role they played in early American life. However, before we can do that, we need to go even further back in time and trace the origins of the right to bear arms.

As you will see, throughout world history, a citizen's right to bear arms went hand in hand with the notions of freedom and democracy.

ARMS IN THE ANCIENT WORLD

More than 2,500 years ago, ancient Greece was made up of many independent city-states. Each city functioned as a tiny country, with its own particular type of government. Back then, Athens was one such city-state with a democratic government in which all free citizens met to discuss how Athens should be run. One important right of Athenians was that all free adult men were allowed to bear arms. Naturally, back in 400 BCE, there were no guns. Instead, Athenians were permitted to bear arms such as shields, spears, and protective metal armor. By law, upon turning eighteen,

Arms have been prominent in nearly all societies as a means of protection against oppressors. This ancient Athenian table shows two armed warriors in combat.

all healthy men had to complete two years of military training. This army made up the first organized militia of which there are written records. Broadly defined, a militia is a group of armed citizens.

Although Athens is known for being a model for modern democracies, it's important to realize that only a small percentage of Athenians were actually considered "free" citizens with full rights. Women, foreigners, and slaves (who made up close to one-third of the population) neither participated in government decisions nor shared citizens' rights, including the right to bear arms. The one exception to this rule was during times of war, when slaves were temporarily granted citizens' rights and were allowed to carry and use arms.

During the same period, the Roman Empire was in full swing and was thriving. Roman law permitted its citizens to keep arms and use them in self-defense. However, bearing a weapon with intent to kill someone was considered a crime. Of course, as in Athens, not everybody was considered a Roman citizen. In fact, membership was even more limited than it was in democratic Athens—it was largely restricted to men born into rich and powerful families.

As in Athens, citizens in Rome were trained in using swords, axes, and bows and arrows for defense. As centuries passed, these wealthy arms-bearing Romans dominated the poor unarmed masses who grew increasingly fed up as they watched the nobles live it up in the lap of luxury. Fearing revolt, this rich and powerful minority formed a permanent militia in order to keep the common people under control. Finally however, to keep the masses happy, in the third century BCE the Roman government gave in and allowed Roman-born men equal voting rights.

In order to expand its empire, Rome waged many battles to conquer new lands. Unfortunately, over the years, many battles—and men—were lost. Needing

MORE THAN A DECADE AFTER THE COLUMBINE MASSACRE

The date was April 20, 1999, yet the effects of that day continue to resonate. And tragically, before the day was over, it had already gone down in history as one of the deadliest school massacres ever to take place in the United States. It all began at 11:21 AM, on a sunny spring morning in the town of Littleton, Colorado. Dressed in dark trench coats, two teenage students stormed into their suburban high school. Armed with shotguns and explosives, they went on a shooting spree that left twelve other students, one teacher, and themselves dead. More than two dozen other people were injured.

The rampage ended only when the two young men turned their guns on themselves. One student, who had been hiding in a closet with a teacher and some friends, said, "I kept thinking to myself, 'This can't be happening to our school.'"

America was shocked by the brutal shootings at Columbine High School. Police, parents, teachers, students, lawmakers, and even the president were forced to reexamine some serious issues about safety, violence, and the role of guns in our lives. What were two teens doing with shotguns? How and where did they get them? Why did they shoot their classmates and teachers before eventually shooting themselves? Could such a shooting have been prevented? If so, how?

Numerous school shootings have occurred since Columbine, including, the shooting that took place on April 16, 2007, at Virginia Polytechnic Institute and State University in Blacksburg, Virginia, which claimed the lives of 32 people and injured many more. The fact that school shootings are still taking place tells us that if there is a way they can be prevented, there's still work to be done.

more manpower, like the Athenians before them, Romans hit on the idea of giving some slaves and foreigners citizens' rights. Doing so allowed them to bear arms in the Roman army (and get killed as well).

THE MIDDLE AGES

In the years between 800 to 1100, western Europe was divided into tiny independent regions; nations came later. Each region was centered around a small fortified town or castle ruled by a powerful, wealthy lord. Lords governed through a system known as feudalism.

Under feudalism, a lord who owned land would allow a number of wealthy noblemen and warriors to become his vassals. Being a lord's vassal meant that these noblemen were allowed to farm parts of the lord's land. In return however, vassals had to assemble armies that would fight for the lord and defend his lands if attacked by invaders. These armies were made up of wealthy noblemen called knights. It was the vassals who provided knights with the necessary arms for battle: swords, bows, arrows, helmets, and armor.

Meanwhile, the ones who did the actual farming were the peasants, or common people. Peasants couldn't become vassals or knights and they couldn't bear arms. Instead of getting paid for their work, the vassals guaranteed them protection from invading enemies. This situation began to change in the twelfth century.

LINE OF PLANTAGENET.

EDWARD III.

In 1328, King Edward III of England signed the Statute of Northampton, which laid the groundwork for some of our gun control laws today.

The brand-new kingdom of England was the place where it all began.

ARMS IN ENGLAND

Over the decades, England's feudal lords lost their power and their kingdoms were united under a single ruler who became king of all of England. In 1181, England's king was Henry II. Under his rule, a law was passed that was the first to deal with the right to bear arms in the kingdom.

The law, called the Assize of Arms, made it obligatory for all free men (the king's vassals) to possess certain types of arms. The number and type of arms each citizen could possess depended on that citizen's wealth and power. The richer and more important you were, the more arms you could have. The reason behind the Assize was that the king would have a militia ready to fight for him at any time. However, these same weapons provided wealthy people with the potential power to overthrow a bad or overly authoritarian king, should they need to do so.

In 1328, King Edward III signed another important arms law. This law, called the Statute of Northampton, was an ancestor to our contemporary gun control laws in that it made it illegal for people to carry weapons in public places: "No man great or small . . . [shall] go nor ride armed by night nor by day . . . upon pain to forfeit their armor to the King and their bodies to prison at the King's pleasure." Like many of our gun control laws today, the aim of the Statute of Northampton was to reduce the high number of murders and robberies. But (like many of our gun control laws today) while law-abiding citizens obeyed the law, crooks and criminals didn't.

In England, only the rich owned guns. Most kings felt the same as Henry VIII. Henry VIII tried to limit ownership of firearms because his army consisted of commoners who fought with powerful armor-piercing longbows. He thought that if they had access to guns, they would stop practicing with bows and arrows and his army would become weaker. By 1541, however, guns had become mainstream and Henry VIII had to give up his fight and allow widespread ownership and use of most firearms.

Guns became very popular during the civil war that raged between 1642 and 1651, in which the English Parliament rebelled against the abusive

In 1885, the Supreme Court heard yet another case that dealt with the Second Amendment. A young Illinois resident named Herman Presser had organized, and led through the streets of Chicago, a small army of four hundred armed German Americans. Although they carried rifles, these men were not part of the state militia or the U.S. Army. An Illinois law made it illegal for armed groups to assemble and parade in public without a permit. Accordingly, Presser was sentenced to pay a $10 fine.

Presser, however, declared this law unconstitutional because it violated his Second Amendment right to bear arms. The Supreme Court disagreed with him and upheld the state law. According to the Court "the amendment is a limitation only upon the power of Congress and the National government, and not upon that of the States."

Although a state could not control the bearing of arms in a way that would infringe upon its militia, the state could make it illegal for citizens to bear arms for reasons that weren't military.

The Court based its ruling on the precedent of *United States v. Cruikshank*: "A State may pass laws to regulate the privileges and immunities of its own citizens, provided that in so doing it does not abridge their privileges and immunities as citizens of the United States." Its decision proved that the Court did not see the right to bear arms as an absolute right of American citizens.

authority of King Charles I. A highly organized militia known as the New Model Army was organized by Parliament. Its soldiers were better fed and better paid than any previous army ever had been. They were disciplined and knew how to use guns. Because of this, the New Model Army, led by the popular hero Oliver Cromwell, defeated the king and his army.

Once the king was booted out of power, Cromwell took over the reigns of governing England. Using his great military (and gun) power, he dissolved Parliament and ruled the country as a military dictator. In order to stifle any revolts, he used his New Model Army to keep the English people in line. Often the military force he used was quite brutal. When Cromwell died in 1658, the English were happy to have their king back again. They never forgot how power—backed up by a ruler's strong army—could be easily abused.

In 1671, under Cromwell's royal successor, King Charles II, Parliament passed a gun control law called the Game Act. This law prohibited the use of guns, bows, and hunting dogs by anybody—whether rich or poor—who didn't own large areas of land. In effect, only wealthy landowners could hunt and therefore only they had the right to own and bear arms. Coincidentally, these wealthy landowners were the citizens whose power had been increasing the most over the last two centuries. At the same time, the law gave

Charles II a nice opportunity to seize the weapons of his potential enemies, thus keeping them disarmed and not dangerous. Other gun control measures imposed by Charles II included a law by which all gunsmiths had to report weekly gun sales, and another by which only those with a license could import weapons into England from abroad.

THE ENGLISH BILL OF RIGHTS

The next king in line after Charles II was James II. Although when he came to power in 1685 he promised to "go as far as any man in preserving [England] in all its just rights and liberties," the English quickly caught on that James II intended nothing of the kind. Fuelled by his desire to make Roman Catholicism the most important religion in the country, James II banned all Protestants from bearing arms. Thumbing his nose at the law, he wouldn't let Protestants serve in the army, hold posts in government, or be employed as judges. Anybody who disagreed with him was put on trial. And to enforce his will, he increased the royal army from five thousand to thirty thousand men.

Not surprisingly, James II didn't win any popularity contests with the people. In fact, even most of his own impressive army refused to fight for him. They turned on him, kicking him out of the country in what came to be known as the Glorious (and bloodless) Revolution of 1688.

James II of England was viewed by his people as an absolute monarch. One way he tried to make Roman Catholicism the national religion was by not allowing Protestants to bear arms, thereby leaving them virtually powerless.

With James II out of the way, Parliament decided that it was time citizens defended their own rights and liberties. Obviously, leaders such as Oliver Cromwell and James II couldn't be trusted to do it for them. As such, a committee of citizens drew up a declaration called the English Bill of Rights. The rights included in this document ranged from limits on cruel and unusual punishment to freedom of speech for members of Parliament.

The English Bill of Rights also tackled the issue of the right to bear arms. Snubbing James II, the document provided a clause that allowed Protestants to bear arms "for their Defense." It also prevented a ruler from getting too powerful by inserting a clause that declared "raising or keeping a Standing army within the Kingdom in time of Peace unless it be with Consent of Parliament is against Law."

The English Bill of Rights would prove to be a major inspiration for another Bill of Rights: that of the newly formed United States of America, ratified exactly one hundred years later. Many of the rights and liberties set down in the English Bill of Rights, including the right to bear arms, would find their way into the American Bill of Rights.

Of course it is hardly surprising that English law and culture would have such a great impact on the founding of the United States. After all, those who arrived to settle America's thirteen colonies in the early 1600s were mostly British subjects, many of whom had been persecuted for one reason or another. When they traveled across the Atlantic in search of liberty, they brought along their British ideas about militias and guns, rights and rulers, and knowledge of the laws that governed these matters. The big difference however was that the untamed America these settlers encountered was a far cry from the orderly England they had left behind.

GUNS COME TO AMERICA

The first colonists to arrive in America found themselves in the middle of a vast wilderness. Everything was different. There was no law and no order. People had to fend for and protect themselves. Suddenly guns were more than just for war or for hunting. Guns became a necessary part of life that settlers needed in order to survive.

While in England only the wealthy were given the right to hunt, in colonial America many people had to hunt just so they could have food in their bellies. Some early settlers spent eight to nine months of the year living solely off the meat of the deer they shot. Consequently, most of the land was open to public hunting.

Colonists depended on guns as a means of protection as well. Most of the time, "protection" meant turning the guns on the Native Americans who had inhabited the Americas for thousands of years before Europeans showed up. When the new settlers arrived in America, most Native Americans greeted them warmly. However, after a few decades of the newcomers' attempts to enslave them, steal their land, burn

In establishing America as a nation, firearms were important not only to fight off the tyranny of an oppressive government, but also to explore the land and wilderness.

down their homes, and massacre any of them who put up a fight, the Native Americans had had enough.

Many fierce battles ensued. Native Americans attacked colonists with bows, arrows, and spears, and colonists fought back with the muskets they had brought with them from Europe. Even twelve-year-old boys knew how to shoot these muskets, and many joined in to help the older men.

The colonists needed all the manpower they could get. The Native Americans were extremely savvy warriors who knew much more about the countryside and its animal inhabitants than did the newcomers. The only thing that kept the colonists from being massacred was their firearms.

Because guns played such a key role in everyday colonial American life, owning and using arms was seen as an automatic and natural right. In fact, some of the colonies' governments even insisted upon their citizens being armed. In 1623, Virginia prohibited its residents from traveling unless they were "well armed." In 1658, each Virginia household was obliged to have a working firearm in the house, and in 1673, the colony began actually buying guns for families that couldn't afford them. Meanwhile, in 1644, Massachusetts began fining any citizen who wasn't armed. And in 1770, Georgia passed a law requiring all citizens to take their guns to church with them.

Until the 1760s, the only place you could find a permanent force of British troops was in the colony of New York. This wasn't very reassuring to non-New Yorkers. Realizing that settlers needed to protect themselves, their homes, and their towns, colonial governments had citizens form militias. These militias became the official army in each colony.

They were responsible for keeping order and for defending residents from Native American attackers.

To stay in practice, several days out of each year, the men in each militia would get together for military and gun drills. Militias included all white men between the ages of sixteen and sixty. In most cases, each man had to supply his own gun and ammunition. However, some towns kept a common stockpile of arms and ammunition.

Even if guns did seem to be everywhere in colonial America, some gun control laws existed. For example, in many towns it was illegal to hunt or shoot in the streets. It was also considered a crime to use a gun to threaten or scare people. There were also laws about who was prohibited from using guns and where firearm use was not allowed.

Unsurprisingly, colonists didn't want to encourage the use of guns among Native Americans. A Virginia law prohibited the sale of arms or ammunition to Native Americans, while Massachusetts would let Native Americans carry firearms only if they had a license. Another population segment colonists didn't want toting arms were the newly imported African slaves. Frightened of possible slave revolts, both Virginia and Pennsylvania passed laws prohibiting slaves from carrying arms without permission from their masters.

A REVOLUTION

To us, colonial America might seem as if it was a totally new and free land, far away from England.

EARLY RIGHTS ESTABLISHED AND UPHELD

The Second Amendment concerns firearms. It states that "a well regulated Militia, being necessary to the security of a free State, the right of the people to keep and bear Arms, shall not be infringed." At the time of this amendment's creation, the right for people to bear arms had already been firmly established in England.

During the reign of various kings, such as England's King Henry II of the twelfth century, English subjects were required to have weapons. Subjects kept weapons to protect the kingdom from foreign invaders. Private weapon ownership and use was allowed if it was in the service of king and country. It was also understood that this use could extend to hunting. There was also a common law giving subjects the right to defend themselves if truly endangered.

America's English forefathers relied upon these laws and understandings in their new world. Court judges interpreted existing and common laws in order to rule in favor of defendants or plaintiffs. These are the two opposing parties in a court case. One such court case amazingly protected the rights of the British during a time when the forefathers were trying to sever ties with England.

However, don't forget that it was a colony. And although American realities were very different, American settlers still had to follow rules dictated by the king of England. As time went by, this became more and more of a problem.

Because the thirteen American colonies were English, their citizens were expected to show loyalty to the king of England. Part of this meant paying taxes. However, as England got itself involved in a series of expensive wars, it needed more and more money to pay for military expenses. To raise this money, England looked to its colonies. Consequently, the taxes imposed on the colonies by the English Parliament grew higher and higher.

After about ten years of these increased taxes, American colonists started to get angry. They resented the fact that they had no representation in Parliament and therefore could not protest the constantly increasing taxes. Instead of addressing their concerns, Parliament continued to smother the colonies with new taxes.

As tensions rose, King George III decided to send British troops to Boston to protect English officials who were being threatened by angry colonists. This British army only made the colonists angrier. They felt that the king had no right to station troops in Boston when there was no war being fought. On March 5, 1770, Boston citizens took to hurling insults, and then rocks, at the British troops. Although the soldiers tried to keep cool, when someone yelled "Fire!" they shot their muskets off into the crowd. Five people were killed in what was soon to be known as the Boston Massacre.

The Boston Massacre was an example of how arms allowed citizens to fight off an oppressive government. In this case, the British Empire was overtaxing the colonists.

Word of the Boston Massacre spread around the colonies like wildfire. Although they still considered themselves the king's subjects, the colonists resented the British troops. They believed that armies in peacetime were dangerous to a democracy. They believed that a better, more democratic means of defense was to use the people themselves, organized into militias as the colonies had been doing.

The conflicts came to a head in 1775. In September 1774, the First Continental Congress had met in Philadelphia, Pennsylvania. Delegates had decided that until England got rid of its abusive tax laws, the colonies would not trade with their mother country. The king refused to lower taxes. Instead he sent more British troops to quash a new rebellion in Massachusetts.

In Boston, Governor Thomas Gage was ordered to take up arms against the rebels. Against his will (he had lived in the colonies for eighteen years and his wife was American), he did his duty and made plans to take the people's arms and ammunition that had been stored at Concord and

Lexington. On April 18, 1775, English troops—called redcoats because of their flaming scarlet uniforms—marched on Concord. Militiamen came out to fight and protect their homes. Suddenly, the American Revolution had begun.

THE FIGHT FOR FREEDOM

The Second Continental Congress was held a couple of weeks after the first shot rang out. Delegates called for the people to "bear arms" and fight the redcoats. However, just fighting was not enough. One of the problems that Congress faced was how to win the revolution. Although the various citizens' militias proved courageous, they lacked the discipline, organization, and experience of the English troops. If America was going to win the war, something had to be done. The solution was to create a Continental army that would organize the various colonies' militias under the command of a man named George Washington.

The Congress also urged each colony to set up its own representative government. In doing so, many of these new "states" drew up their own Bill of Rights. Among the rights guaranteed in many of these documents was the right to bear arms. The Virginia Declaration of Rights, for example, went like this: "A well regulated militia, composed of the body of the people, trained to arms, is the proper, natural, and safe

The U.S. Constitution is considered the nation's most important document. It is displayed in the National Archives building in Washington, D.C.

defense of a free state." Other states with similar statements were Vermont, Pennsylvania, Massachusetts, and North Carolina.

Only a year into the American Revolution, the colonists were already firmly decided that they wanted a definite split from England. The result was the Declaration of Independence, drafted by fifty-six members of the Continental Congress. On July 4,

1776, Congress president John Hancock was the first to sign this historic document. The Declaration of Independence listed many of the colonies' major complaints against the king of England before going on to declare: "These United Colonies are, and of Right ought to be Free and Independent States; that they are Absolved from all Allegiance to the British Crown." When the last of the fifty-six delegates had signed the declaration, the United States of America was born.

American troops were motivated by their newly declared independence and now, unified as the Continental Army, were much more efficient. Nonetheless, the Revolutionary War raged for another five years. Finally however, the British surrendered to General George Washington in October 1781. On September 3, 1783, the Treaty of Paris, signed by both nations, officially granted the United States independence from Great Britain.

THE BIRTH OF THE
SECOND AMENDMENT

Winning the Revolutionary War was a great victory for both the United States of America and for democracy. However, once the treaties had been signed and the soldiers had returned to their homes, some big questions remained to be answered. What kind of new government would this new nation have? How much independence would be given to each of the country's thirteen states? What rights and responsibilities could citizens depend upon? And what would be the role of guns?

When the war ended in 1781, the thirteen states were not like the states we know today. Instead, each was like its own little country. States had their own independent governments and Bills of Rights, their own laws, their own militia, and even their own money. And many of them liked this independence. Although they had banded together to beat the British, once the common enemy was gone, each state was content to go its own way and look out for its own interests. Of course, almost immediately, these interests came into conflict with one another. Economic and trade disputes broke out.

The Declaration of Independence officially freed the thirteen American colonies from British rule.

Some members of the Continental Congress felt that drawing up a federal constitution would bring together the different states in a strong and harmonious union. If this wasn't possible, it was doubtful whether the new nation could survive.

THE ARTICLES OF CONFEDERATION

In 1776, after drawing up and signing the Declaration of Independence, the members of the Second

Continental Congress set to work designing a plan for the new nation's government. The results of this tough task were the Articles of Confederation.

One reason the task was so tough was that many of the future states' delegates refused to approve certain clauses in the document. They were worried about a central or federal government having too much power. Because of this, five years of disputes and debates went by before all thirteen states approved the Articles of Confederation in 1781.

However, by the time all the states had finished with it, the final document had created a federal government with very little power. The national government had no executive branch (a president) and no federal court system. It had no authority to control trade between the states and could tax the states only if they agreed to be taxed. Furthermore, the new government would have no right to form a national army—the states all fiercely opposed this. Each wanted to continue with its own militia. The oppressive years of English rule had left a bad taste in their mouths. Instead of giving up their power, they wanted citizens to be able to bear arms and fight against any central government that began abusing its power.

The years between 1781 and 1788 proved how insubstantial the Articles of Confederation were. In order to pay debts accumulated from the Revolutionary War, states taxed each other but many of these taxes went unpaid. Rebellions broke out and disputes over trade issues were common. Economically, things became chaotic. Furthermore, Congress soon realized that it couldn't count on state militias to fight federal battles. One of the events that led to this realization was Shays's Rebellion.

In 1786, a Massachusetts farmer named Daniel Shays led a group of several hundred armed men into the state capital of Springfield. Shays and his followers were protesting because the local economy was severely depressed and they were unable to pay off their debts. Because of this, their farms were being taken away from them. The group invaded the state supreme court and forced it to close down. In doing so, they stopped the legal proceedings that were going to take away their farms.

This and other uprisings made some members of Congress nervous. It made them realize that if the nation was to defend itself from armed groups both inside and outside of the country, it would need a stronger and more permanent military force than the local state militias could provide. They concluded that the way things were going, without a stronger federal government and a strong national army, the future of the United States of America was at stake. Hoping to resolve the situation, two members of Congress, James Madison of Virginia and Alexander Hamilton of New York, invited delegates from all of the states to a

The signing of the Constitution in 1787 laid the groundwork for the gun rights we continue to have today. Among the priorities was to not allow one group to hold too much power over another group.

convention scheduled to begin May 14, 1787, in Philadelphia.

FORGING A NEW CONSTITUTION

The weather that spring of 1787 was so terrible that it took many state delegates a long time to get to Philadelphia. Hence, instead of beginning on May 14, the Constitutional Convention began on May 25. Representatives from twelve states made it to the convention. The one "no show" was rebellious Rhode

Island, which liked the Articles of Confederation fine the way they were.

Throughout the long, hot summer of 1787, the fifty-five delegates—later known as the Founding Fathers—met at Independence Hall and debated how to successfully govern the United States. The delegates began by laying down some ground rules. George Washington, hero of the American Revolution, would be their chairman. Each state would have one vote and only one vote. And everything discussed at the convention was top secret. The press was kept in the dark. Security guards were hired to chase away spies and eavesdroppers. Delegates were not even allowed to write home to talk about what was going on. Although some delegates got fed up and left, most stuck around to help write the new constitution that became the country's bible. The constitution that they finally hammered out is the same one we still use today.

Among the many decisions the Founding Fathers made was how to organize the new federal government. Power would be shared between an executive branch (the president), a legislative branch (Congress), and a judicial branch (the courts). Such a division ensured that no one branch could become too powerful and abuse the people's rights. If one branch got out of hand, there were always the other two branches to keep it in line. This system came to be known as one of checks and balances.

Congress was made up of two houses. One house, called the House of Representatives, would have representatives from all states. The number of representatives would be based on a state's population. Virginia, for instance, being one of the most populated states at the time, had more representatives than the less populated state of New Jersey. The other house, called the Senate, would have an equal number of representatives from each state. In other words, both Virginia, New Jersey (which had a small population), and every other state would each send two senators to Congress. Congress's powers would include passing laws, raising taxes, regulating the national economy, and declaring war. It could raise and support an army or navy and summon state militias to defend against rebellions and invasions.

The president's job was to carry out the laws Congress passed, make decisions about foreign affairs, and command the military. Meanwhile it was up to the federal courts to reject laws passed by Congress or the state governments that federal judges believed were contrary to laws or rights set down in the Constitution.

In the same way that power was balanced between executive, legislative, and judicial branches, it was also divided between the federal government and the state governments. Some of the Founding Fathers, known as Federalists, believed that a strong

When Congress passed the National Firearms Act of 1934, there was much opposition from those who claimed that it was unconstitutional for the federal government to infringe upon the people's rights guaranteed in the Second Amendment. The issue came up in court soon after, when Jack Miller and Frank Layton were charged with transporting a sawed-off double-barrel shotgun from one state to another without the registration and tax stamp required by the Firearms Act. A federal district court had set Miller and Layton free, arguing that the federal law violated the Second Amendment.

For the first and only time in its history, the Supreme Court was faced with the issue of a federal law that potentially limited Second Amendment rights. In a historic decision, the Court overruled the district court and upheld the federal law. The Supreme Court argued that the National Firearms Act did not violate the Second Amendment because the Second Amendment did not specifically protect the right to own and use weapons that were not useful to militias. The Court said that there was no "evidence tending to show that possession or use of a 'shotgun having a barrel of less than eighteen inches in length' at this time has some reasonable relationship to the preservation or efficiency of a well regulated militia, we cannot say that the Second Amendment guarantees the right to keep and bear such an instrument."

Although the Court argued that the right to bear arms is a collective right related to militia service, it did not express an opinion concerning the Second Amendment and the individual's right to bear arms.

Since then, there have been a number of Supreme Court interpretations of *United States v. Miller*,

including *Konigsberg v. State Bar* (1961), *Atlanta Motel v. United States* (1961), *Adams v. Williams* (1972), *Lewis v. United States* (1980), *Printz v. United States* (1997), and *District of Columbia v. Heller* (2008).

federal government was necessary to bind the country together. Because of their arguments, the Constitution put the federal government in charge of the national economy, relations with foreign countries, and military affairs. Other Founding Fathers were worried about the states losing too much autonomy. These Anti-Federalists felt that in many cases the states themselves knew best about certain local issues. Their positions were reflected in a Constitution that decided to let states run their own economies, organize and train their own militias, and make many of their own laws.

SIGNING THE CONSTITUTION

Getting the Constitution signed by all the delegates proved to be a difficult process. The biggest stumbling block was the Anti-Federalists. Many feared that the Constitution gave too much power to the federal government at the states' expense. They feared that such a government might abuse the people's rights just as the

English government had. Anti-Federalist Founding Father George Mason of Virginia said that he would sooner chop off his right hand than use it to sign the Constitution.

Other Anti-Federalists agreed with him. What many wanted was a Bill of Rights that would safeguard the rights and liberties of the citizens and the states. Although he was in France at the time (serving as ambassador), Thomas Jefferson, author of the Declaration of Independence and future third president, wrote a letter to his friend and Founding Father James Madison, in which he said "A bill of rights is what the people are entitled to against every government on earth."

Although Federalists thought that the Constitution was fine as it was, they realized that without a Bill of Rights, the Anti-Federalist delegates wouldn't sign it and the states wouldn't accept it. For this reason, they agreed to support a Bill of Rights that would be added to the Constitution at a later date. With this assurance, on September 17, 1787, thirty-nine delegates approved the new Constitution. Thirteen others had already gone home, and only three delegates refused to sign at all. One of these was Anti-Federalist George Mason.

Of course, the constitutional battle was far from being over. Although the delegates had approved it, the Constitution had to be ratified, or approved, by at

The Federalist, later called the Federalist Papers, was published in 1788 and argued for the ratification of the Constitution.

least nine out of thirteen states before being adopted as the law of the land.

Founding Fathers James Madison, Alexander Hamilton, and John Jay wrote arguments in support of the Constitution. Called the Federalist Papers, these were published in the country's main newspapers in an attempt to get state support for the Constitution. Echoing the Anti-Federalists' arguments, many states were afraid that the Constitution gave too much power to the federal government. They wanted guarantees that protected citizens' basic rights and liberties, such as the right to free speech and the right to free press. One of the most important freedoms that they felt the Constitution didn't address was the individual's right to bear arms. The writers of the Constitution argued that ownership and use of guns was such a natural part of American life that it was taken for granted that the people could keep and bear arms. However, individual states, many of whose governments possessed a Bill of Rights that specifically upheld their citizens' right to bear arms, wanted this and other rights to be set down in black and white.

Once assurances were made that the right to bear arms and other fundamental individual liberties would be included in a Bill of Rights that would be amended, or added, to the Constitution, the states eventually came around one by one. Although they had fought for a clause stating that "Congress shall never disarm any citizen, unless such as are or have been in actual rebellion," Delaware was the first of the thirteen states to ratify the Constitution. Even though many states had similar amendments concerning the right to bear arms, almost all of them approved the Constitution as well. (The two holdouts were North Carolina and Rhode Island. North Carolina ratified the Constitution in November of 1789 and Rhode Island

The Bill of Rights, which includes the Second Amendment right to bear arms, serves as the cornerstone of the Constitution, limiting the power of the federal government over the states.

in May of 1790.) Amidst much celebrating, in June 1788, the Constitution became the law of the land.

THE SECOND AMENDMENT AND THE BILL OF RIGHTS

No sooner had the festivities died down than the Founding Fathers were back at the drawing board. This time they went to work creating the Bill of

Rights they had promised to the Anti-Federalists and the states. James Madison was the one who actually did most of the writing of the amendments to the Constitution. He originally penned seventeen, but these were whittled down to the ten amendments that were accepted and that still exist today.

Among the rights that the Bill of Rights guaranteed were free speech; freedom of the press; freedom to practice all religions; freedom to meet in public; freedom against unreasonable searches and seizures in one's home; the right to a speedy, public trial by jury; the right to an attorney when accused of a crime; the right to reasonable bail; no cruel or unusual punishment; and no requirement to house soldiers in one's home during peacetime. The states were satisfied by the Tenth Amendment, which automatically assured them power over all matters not granted to the federal government in the Constitution. And everybody seemed satisfied by the Second Amendment, concerning the right to bear arms.

Madison labored a long time over the wording of the Second Amendment. Seeking inspiration, he turned to the English Bill of Rights of 1689 as well as looked at many of the early bills of rights written by the individual American colonies. Many of these state bills of rights granted the people as a whole the right to bear arms for the defense of the state and recognized the right of individual citizens to bear arms. However, the two Declarations of Rights that influenced Madison the most were Virginia's and Pennsylvania's.

Written by George Mason in 1776, Virginia's Declaration of Rights stated:

> That a well-regulated militia, composed of the body of the people, trained to arms, is the proper, natural and safe defense of a free State; that standing armies, in time of peace, should be avoided, as dangerous to liberty.

Penned the same year, the Pennsylvania Declaration of Rights declared:

> That the people have a right to bear arms for the defense of themselves and the state; and as standing armies in the time of peace are dangerous to liberty, they ought not to be kept up.

From these models, Madison came up with the following rough draft of the Second Amendment:

> The right of the people to keep and bear arms shall not be infringed; a well armed and well regulated militia being the best security of a free

country: but no person religiously scrupulous of bearing arms shall be compelled to render military service in person.

He submitted this draft to Congress, where its wording was much discussed. Eventually the amendment was approved, but the final clause about religious scruples was removed. This is because some members of Congress believe it gave some people an excuse to avoid military service. In the end, the Second Amendment consisted of twenty-seven words:

A well regulated Militia, being necessary to the security of a free State, the right of the people to keep and bear Arms, shall not be infringed.

On September 25, 1789, this and eleven other amendments were adopted by Congress. By December 15, 1791, the necessary number of states had ratified ten of these amendments. These ten, including the Second Amendment, became the Bill of Rights.

FIREARMS IN THE NINETEENTH CENTURY

The United States of America entered the nineteenth century as a free country, its citizens proud and protective of their hard-won liberties. One of these liberties was the people's right to bear arms. In fact, the people had won these liberties because they bore arms. So you can imagine how important this right was to early Americans as they set to work building a new nation.

The United States in 1800 was a much smaller, weaker, and less wealthy nation than it is today. Most of the Midwest and the western states were still largely undiscovered and unsettled.

In the early years of the nineteenth century, French emperor Napoléon Bonaparte was hard at war, invading and adding various European countries to his empire. Fearful that Napoléon's imperial dreams might cause him to cross the Atlantic, nervous American gun manufacturers started increasing the production of guns.

Not only did the quantity of firearms manufactured increase, but the quality did as well. In fact, by the middle of the century, American

As Americans were moving westward in the 1800s, fire-arms became a necessary part of life for both protection and hunting.

military arms were considered to be the best in the world. American manufacturers were exporting their wares to countries all over the world. Meanwhile at home, as guns became more available and more afford-able, Americans were buying them up like never before.

Throughout the nineteenth century guns remained a central part of American culture. Hunting and target shooting were the most popular outdoor sports. And dueling was often used to resolve arguments.

Then, of course, there was the West to be won. The nineteenth century marked America's great expansion across the plains to the Pacific. To the pioneers and settlers who journeyed west, guns were as essential as they had been to the first colonists who arrived in the New World. Guns put food on the table. They also allowed settlers to protect themselves from Native American attackers.

The native peoples were not pleased at having newcomers seize their lands and encroach on their hunting grounds. They put up a fight, meaning that ambushes, battles, and massacres between settlers and Native Americans became commonplace throughout the American West. The conflicts only came to a halt in 1890, with the defeat of Chief Big Foot and the last free tribe of Lakotas at the Battle of Wounded Knee, in South Dakota.

THE GOLD RUSH

In 1849, the discovery of gold in California drew thousands and thousands of settlers to the West. Knowing how important guns would be to their survival, Congress went as far as to pass an 1849 law that provided free army weapons to the new residents of California, Oregon, and New Mexico. In doing so, the government endorsed the individual's right to bear arms. Congress knew that without any police or

Even though the right to bear arms was explicitly stated in the Constitution, African Americans and Native Americans were not legally permitted to possess firearms.

militia to protect them, each citizen would have to look out for himself.

As a result, guns and gun culture became and important part of the far West experience. Wearing a loaded gun in the street was just like donning a hat and putting on a pair of boots. As the century wore on and small towns sprung up, local governments tried to enforce some law and order in an attempt to prevent the many public shootouts that had become commonplace. However, the typical response was not unlike that of a small Texas frontier town. When law officials posted notices that prohibited carrying guns, the local boys promptly shot holes through the notices. For a long time life in the West was just like in the westerns. How fast you could draw was more important than the law.

Meanwhile, back east the situation was much different. A far cry from an untamed wilderness, the eastern states were rapidly urbanizing. Cities were growing at an accelerated rate. Nobody needed to hunt much of anything, and most of the Native Americans were dead or had gone elsewhere. This made it pretty pointless to haul around a big rifle. The only guns that were sometimes carried were small pistols or revolvers. Known as handguns, these were used for self-protection and were kept hidden from view. In general however, most eastern city residents didn't walk around with guns.

The Boston Massacre

The Boston Massacre was a disturbance between some local settlers and British soldiers on March 5, 1770. The British had a strong presence in Boston. The locals resented their presence and did not like doing business with them. A local began taunting one of the soldiers. The argument soon drew an angry mob and turned to mayhem. The soldiers fired their muskets into the crowd, killing five Bostonians. John Adams represented the British soldiers involved in the Boston Massacre in court.

John Adams argued that the British soldiers were endangered and therefore had the right to defend themselves against the locals. The charge against them was that they were acting maliciously with intent to murder the colonists. The command "Fire!" was heard, which may have caused the soldiers to fire into the crowd. The commanding officer testified that he did not give the order to fire. He told his men to hold their fire.

Six of the soldiers were acquitted of the charges and set free. Two of the soldiers were found guilty of manslaughter. Manslaughter is when a person causes the death of another under any of the following circumstances:

- While under extreme emotional disturbance
- While acting recklessly
- While believing that under the circumstances, there is a justification or reason for it

The six soldiers who were set free were innocent of manslaughter. The interpretation of the circumstances was that they acted accordingly. Even though the colonists were victims of possibly unwarranted gun violence, the soldiers' rights to self-defense were protected.

The firearms that were used in the East were being used increasingly by criminals. As more and more people moved to industrializing cities, there was a surge of violence and crime, riots and strikes. The fact that crooks and mobs took to using guns made American cities dangerous places and made American citizens fearful of guns ending up in the wrong hands. A few citizens began calling for some type of gun control so that they could walk the streets safely.

GUNS AND CITIZENSHIP

Whether you lived in the Wild West or in the urban East, throughout the nineteenth century every American citizen had the right to bear arms. Most American citizens took full advantage of this right. And they had the full support of local, state, and federal governments to do so.

Of course, there were those who didn't have such rights because they weren't considered U.S. citizens. Although America was supposedly a democracy, democratic liberties were not extended to either African Americans or Native Americans. In terms of African Americans, this view became official on March 6, 1857. On this date, the U.S. Supreme Court ruled that blacks, whether free or slaves, were not entitled to the rights set down in the Constitution and Bill of Rights. Known as the *Dred Scott* case, this ruling by the judicial branch of the federal government made it clear

Even though African Americans weren't granted the right to bear arms early on, many used firearms to fight in the Civil War. Those soldiers are memorialized in the *Spirit of Freedom* statue in Washington, D.C.

that blacks had "no rights which any white man was bound to respect." Such rights included the right to bear arms.

Interestingly, although blacks were forbidden from owning and carrying arms, the federal government was happy to make an exception when the Civil War broke out in 1861. In the North, at first only white volunteers were allowed to join the Union army. However, when not enough white men volunteered, Congress passed the Militia Act of July 1862. The act required all males between eighteen and forty-five to fight for the Union. This included black males as well, who formed their own regiments. All in all, over two hundred thousand black Americans fought for the Union during the Civil War. Of these, thirty-eight thousand lost their lives. As its losses grew, even the Confederate South was ready to let slaves do some fighting. But by the time a Confederate law had been passed that allowed blacks to fight, it was too late. The Union had already won the war. Some believe

that the Yankees' victory was partly due to the added manpower and fighting skills of the black soldiers.

Of course, one of the good things to come out of the end of the Civil War was the end of slavery. In 1865, the Thirteenth Amendment was passed, prohibiting all forms of slavery in the United States. This was followed by the passing of the Civil Rights Act in 1866. The Civil Rights Act was the first law to declare that "all persons born in the United States and not subject to any foreign power" were American citizens. As such, these citizens "of every race and color" could enjoy the "full and equal benefit of all laws and proceedings for the security of person and property, as is enjoyed by white citizens."

The federal government had recognized that, in terms of black Americans, such rights—including the right to bear arms—were necessary. Whether they were free or not, blacks needed to protect themselves. Even after the Civil War and the passing of the Civil Rights Act, black Americans were often lynched, hanged, shot, or burned by angry white mobs—for the most part Southerners. Instead of coming to their defense, white militias in the South were often responsible for such racist attacks. Frederick Douglass, the former slave who was one of the great leaders in the fight to end slavery, publicly encouraged black Americans to own and use guns to defend themselves.

In spite of the Civil Rights Act—which in 1866 officially became a part of the Constitution when its contents were ratified as the Fourteenth Amendment—the white militias of many Southern states continued to invade black homes and seize their guns. Furthermore, governments of many Southern states passed state laws known as "black codes" that prohibited blacks from keeping or carrying any type of firearm.

The states argued that the Bill of Rights applied only to laws passed by the federal government and not to the states. This view was upheld by the Supreme Court in 1876 when a case known as *United States v. Cruikshank* was heard. The case questioned whether it was constitutional to prevent blacks from legally bearing arms. The Court's interpretation was that such questions were up to individual states, not the federal government. Until the Court changed its interpretation, in many states black Americans would not be allowed to own or use guns until well into the early twentieth century.

Other "have-nots" were Native Americans. In 1835, President Andrew Jackson began a national policy of expelling Native Americans from their lands in the East and giving the land to newly arrived white settlers. Native Americans were herded out west onto plots of lands called reservations. In return for moving, the government equipped the Native Americans

Native Americans, such as this Seminole chief, were forced westward onto reservations and were often given firearms in exchange for their land.

with "arms, ammunition, and other indispensable items." They were supplied with steel and iron and taught to be gunsmiths.

Of course, as Native Americans became armed, settlers out west became increasingly unhappy. They still feared attacks from their traditional enemies. As a result of such complaints, Congress passed a law in 1876 banning the sale of certain types of ammunition to "hostile Indians" in certain western states. Obviously, without ammunition Native Americans couldn't use most of the guns being manufactured at the time. Things became more difficult after the Supreme Court, in 1884, ruled that Native Americans, even those who left their tribes and lived with whites, were not American citizens and therefore could not bear arms. In fact, Native Americans would have to wait until 1924 before they officially became U.S. citizens and until 1979 before they received the same right to bear arms as other Americans.

LEGISLATING GUNS

It would be safe to say that prior to the twentieth century, life in America was probably a lot simpler. The United States was a smaller country with a smaller population. There was less technology, diversity, and complexity. There were not as many options, and there were fewer choices to make.

The twentieth century brought with it many changes. And these changes had great effects on American society and culture. They also had a great effect on how Americans used and viewed guns. By the end of the 1800s, the final frontier had been tamed and industrialization was predominant. People no longer needed guns in order to survive, but the large number of guns being produced were more accurate and sophisticated than ever before. In the many new and quickly growing cities, the birth of organized police forces meant that citizens no longer had to rely on guns to protect themselves. They certainly didn't need guns to kill deer for dinner or shoot "hostile" Native Americans. What, then, were guns being used for?

Increasingly, they were being used for purposes that were less essential and more destructive. In the rapidly expanding cities, economic depression and unemployment led to strikes, riots, and criminal activity. Unfortunately, guns played a big part in this new urban violence. More and more, guns were used to kill and maim, not just to defend one's person, property, or country. In fact, the entire country went into shock when President William McKinley was assassinated by a deranged anarchist in 1901. This event was a sign of things to come throughout the rest of the century. The result was that frightened Americans, confronted with daily holdups and shoot-outs in the streets, began thinking twice about the right to bear arms. If nobody disputed the actual right, people criticized the easy availability of these dangerous weapons.

The changes in American society and in the role of guns in this society would not only affect the views of private citizens, but those of federal and state governments, lawmakers, and courts. Throughout the nineteenth century nobody challenged either the Second Amendment or the people's unlimited right to bear arms. However, in the twentieth century, interpretation of this fundamental liberty would become a major source of debate between those who believed gun control was necessary and their opponents who felt that gun control infringed upon the sacred constitutional rights spelled out in the Second Amendment.

THE FIRST LAWS

Public concern over gun-related violence at the beginning of the twentieth century quickly led to the creation of the first gun control laws. Various state governments felt that it was necessary to regulate or prohibit ownership and use of certain types of arms as a measure of public safety. For example, in 1907, Texas placed a large tax on gun merchants that made it more expensive to buy arms.

In 1913, Oregon passed a law prohibiting anyone without a license from purchasing a handgun. And in 1911, a much-hyped string of shootings in New York City led the state of New York to pass a law that made it a serious crime, or felony, to carry, or even keep, any concealed firearm without a permit. Known as the Sullivan Law, this was the first time in American history that a law regulated not only the right to carry firearms, but the right to buy and keep them as well. When police started arresting people with guns that were all of a sudden illegal, many people protested (unsuccessfully) that their fundamental rights, guaranteed by the Second Amendment, were being abused. Nonetheless, by the end of the 1920s, seventeen other states had passed similar gun control laws.

Meanwhile, around the country, it seemed that violent crime and strikes pitting gun-toting workers, bosses, and police against each other were out of control. In 1919, the first federal attempt at regulating gun ownership occurred with the passage of the War Revenue Act. To pay off federal debts racked up during World War I, the act placed a 10 percent tax on the sale of firearms. Although this law was a small measure, it was only the beginning. During the 1920s, hundreds of laws regulating the sale and ownership of guns were introduced into Congress. Although most didn't get too far, one that did was the Miller Bill.

During the 1920s and 1930s, crime grew much worse in the United States. Prohibition—which made the production, sale, and consumption of all alcohol illegal—was responsible for creating a dangerous underground world of illegal liquor trafficking. Then came the Great Depression, during which one out of four Americans was unemployed, poor, and desperate. Gun-related violence was worse than ever before as gangsters like Al Capone took to using brutal new weapons such as sawed-off shotguns, silencers, and machine guns. Since there was no reason any law-abiding citizen would ever need to bear such arms, terrorized Americans demanded that the government do something about these "gangster weapons."

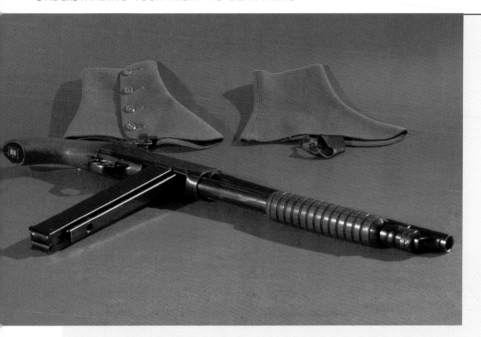

In the early twentieth century, exceedingly powerful firearms, such as this one used by crime boss Al Capone, were becoming an increasing problem, inspiring new debates about the Second Amendment.

In response to this public outcry, Congress passed the National Firearms Act on June 26, 1934. This was the first federal law ever passed by Congress that actually restricted the keeping and bearing of arms. Fearing that the Supreme Court would rule that an actual federal gun control law was unconstitutional under the Second Amendment, the law was proposed as part of a tax bill aimed at taxing the sale of certain firearms. By placing a $200 tax and a registration requirement on the "gangster weapons" mentioned above, the government hoped to make it very difficult for private citizens to own such guns. Furthermore, makers, importers, and dealers of guns would have to pay registration fees to the federal treasury for such weapons, as well as keeping records of their sales.

The follow-up to this law was the Federal Firearms Act of 1938. This act obliged all makers and dealers of firearms to have a license. It also prohibited guns from being sold from one state to another and made it illegal to sell guns to criminals and to those charged with having committed a crime. Overall, the Federal Firearms Act gave the federal government even more power to regulate the sale and possession of guns. In doing so, it revealed the government's belief that restricting sale and ownership of guns did not conflict with the Second Amendment's right to bear arms.

WORLD WAR II

Although World War II broke out in 1939, the United States entered the war only when the Japanese bombed Pearl Harbor, Hawaii, on December 7, 1941. With such an enormous demand for arms worldwide, the American weapons industry was cranking out more arms than ever before. Though the war ended in 1945, America's weapons industry actually stepped up arms production once peace had been declared. After all, during the war years plants had expanded, jobs had been created, and big money was being made. Nobody wanted the boom to stop. Even the federal

PRINTZ V. UNITED STATES

The Brady Act was passed into law in 1993. Of course, just because it became law doesn't mean that the opposition gave up. The Brady Law imposed a five-day waiting period on all handgun purchases. During this waiting period, the law required state or local police to do background checks on the purchasers. Jay Printz, a Montana sheriff, refused to do this background check. He felt that the federal government had no right to tell a local sheriff what to do and to add to his responsibilities without paying him more.

When the Supreme Court heard this case in 1997, it agreed that the part of the Brady Act that required officers to do background checks was unconstitutional. Referring to the Tenth Amendment, which declares that all authority not given to the federal government belongs to the states, the majority sided with Printz. However, even though officers were no longer required to do background checks, the part of the Brady Act that required a five-day waiting period still remained in effect. The minority, who had supported the Brady Act in its entirety, believed that Congress did in fact have authority to respond to escalating gun violence. They quoted a Department of Justice report claiming that "between 1994 and 1996, approximately 6,600 firearms sales each month to potentially dangerous persons were prevented by Brady Act checks; over 70 percent of the rejected purchasers were convicted or indicted felons."

Ultimately, the Supreme Court has been very cautious about interpreting the Second Amendment. Because of this it has heard very few cases that directly concern the exact meaning of the controversial right to bear arms. What the Court has done is to declare that the Second Amendment does not give an individual citizen the absolute right to bear arms. State, local, and federal governments can all pass laws that restrict the individual possession or use of firearms. And these laws are not considered unconstitutional. Of course, there are many laws that are never judged by the Supreme Court. As was mentioned before, most of the twenty thousand gun control laws in existence are state and local laws, which vary from place to place. It is logical, therefore, that their legality is often questioned, and ruled upon, in state courts.

Though *Printz v. United States* was a ruling on the Second Amendment, it also acts as a precedent in the ongoing debate over the power of the federal government over the states. Since the terrorist attacks of September 11, 2001, the power of the federal government to pursue terrorists at the expense of the freedom of individual citizens has been closely watched and debated, and *Printz v. United States* acts as an example that the federal government cannot have unlimited power over states in its efforts to combat crime.

government was making money selling surplus weapons after the war.

American soldiers who came back from fighting returned home with their guns and military training, as well as a keen interest in all types of weapons. Guns were a symbol of victory, freedom, and democracy. Throughout the late 1940s and early 1950s, gun culture flourished in America like never before. All of this changed, however, one bright sunny morning in Dallas, Texas. The date was November 22, 1963. As the young and popular President John F. Kennedy rode by the crowds in his open car, a man named Lee Harvey Oswald gunned him down.

The entire nation was shocked by this brutal assassination. Many have since said that it was the day America lost its innocence. The assassination, captured on film, deeply shocked Americans. The whole nation was suddenly confronted with some negative aspects of its gun culture, specifically the tragic consequences of uncontrolled ownership and use of arms. The fact that Oswald had purchased his Italian rifle from a mail-order catalog enraged many Americans. They felt that there ought to be more control over who owned guns and how they got them in the first place. A week after President Kennedy's death, close to twenty gun control bills had been introduced in Congress. And a major debate was being waged over the true meaning of the Second Amendment. On one hand, there were those who supported gun control. Their interpretation of the Second Amendment followed that of House Representative John Lindsay of New York:

Today the Nation no longer depends on the citizen's weapon, nor does the citizen himself. And, most significant, the population is now densely

LIFE

LEE
OSWALD

with the
weapons he
used to kill
President Kennedy
and
Officer Tippit

FEBRUARY 21 · 1964 · 25¢

Some feel that tighter gun control laws could have prevented Lee Harvey Oswald from assassinating President John F. Kennedy on November 22, 1963, in Dallas, TX.

packed into urban areas, and it is diverse and mobile. In our changed and complicated society, guns have become more dangerous, and they demand more careful use. The Constitution must be interpreted in the light of the times; protection today means the reasonable regulation of firearms—not the absence of regulation.

On the other hand were those who opposed gun control. They felt that such measures threatened the basic individual liberties set out by the Founding Fathers in the Constitution. Their interpretation of the Second Amendment was summed up by Congressman John J. Flynt Jr.:

One of the prized possessions of Americans has been the right to own and possess firearms and to use these firearms in defense of country, in defense of home, in self-defense, provided that use is done in a legal and legitimate manner. The attitude toward firearms has become a historical tradition in the United States. I think it is safe to say that it represents a priceless freedom won by those preceding us as Americans, which few if any other nations enjoy.

Although these gun control bills generated a lot of debate, none of them ultimately became law because of the strong arguments of those who opposed any form of gun regulation. However, throughout the 1960s, opinion polls showed that more than 70 percent of Americans supported stricter gun control laws. While the federal government was loath to react to these figures, between 1965 and 1968 many state governments did pass gun laws. Particularly strict ones were passed in cities such as New York, Chicago, and Philadelphia.

In 1968, two more assassinations of important public figures once again rocked the nation. On April 4, beloved civil rights leader Martin Luther King Jr. was gunned down on the balcony of his motel room in Memphis, Tennessee. Shortly after, on June 5, presidential candidate Robert F. Kennedy (younger brother of John) was killed by a pistol in a Los Angeles hotel.

This time, Congress quickly passed the Gun Control Act of 1968. Replacing the Federal Firearms Act of 1938, this law placed more restrictions on sales of guns between states (handguns, for instance, could not be purchased out of state) and required all gun dealers to keep records of the people to whom they sold weapons in case the police wanted to check on them. It prohibited all sales of guns through the mail as well as all sales of rifles, shotguns, and ammunition to minors under the age of eighteen. Certain people, such as felons and the mentally ill, were prohibited from owning firearms. Those who could buy guns had to sign a statement saying that they were qualified to

John F. Kennedy's brother Robert Kennedy was also murdered by means of a firearm on June 6, 1968, in Los Angeles, California, by assassin Sirhan Sirhan.

do so. Finally, those who violated any of the above conditions could have their guns automatically taken away from them.

In order to avoid accusations that the law was contrary to the Second Amendment, the Gun Control Act of 1968 took care to state that its true aim was to help cut down on crime and violence. The act had no intention of "discouraging or eliminating the private ownership or use of firearms by law-abiding citizens for lawful purposes... [such as] hunting, trapshooting, target shooting, personal protection, or any other lawful activity." In spite of such assurances, gun control opponents were unhappy due to what they viewed as the biggest federal restriction ever on the rights of American gun owners.

Even with the Gun Control Act of 1968 in place, gun-related crimes and violence in the United States only escalated throughout the 1960s and 1970s. And even though many other gun control laws were proposed to Congress—in 1976 alone, there were more than 200 bills dealing with some form of federal gun control—those who opposed gun control were increasingly influential. This became apparent in 1981. On March 30 of that year, President Ronald Reagan was shot in the chest with a bullet from a cheap, poorly made handgun known as a Saturday night special. Although nobody was killed, the president and three other people were wounded. Injured

When an assassination attempt was made on President Ronald Reagan on March 30, 1981, press secretary James Brady was hit in the head, leaving him permanently disabled and inspiring him to become an advocate for gun control laws.

the worst was the president's press secretary, James S. Brady. A shot in the head led to Brady being permanently brain damaged.

In response to this shooting, a handgun crime control bill was introduced into Congress. It prohibited the sale of Saturday night specials and enforced a twenty-one-day wait on any handgun purchases. Pawnshops could not sell guns and anyone convicted of a serious crime committed with a handgun would have to serve a minimum jail sentence of five years. Even with the population up in arms over increased gun-related violence, gun control opponents such as the National Rifle Association fought hard against the bill. In the end, the bill didn't even make it to the voting stage.

In fact, restrictions on gun ownership were actually reduced the next time Congress passed a law related to guns. The 1986 Firearms Owners' Protection Act made it even easier to own a gun. Overturning previous restrictions, it was now possible to purchase a rifle or shotgun in another state and through the mail. It once again became possible to carry (unloaded) weapons from one state to another. Gun dealers didn't have to do as much record keeping of sales as they had before. And a gun could no longer be taken from its owner without a court hearing. The NRA hailed this new law as "the most historic piece of pro-gun regulation ever enacted."

Nonetheless, as the twentieth century came to a close, Congress did pass some significant gun control laws. In 1986, it became a crime for any individual to own a machine gun (those who had purchased theirs before 1986 could hold on to them, however). It also became illegal to sell or use "cop-killer" bullets. Ordinary bullets are made from lead. Cop-killer bullets are made from harder metals such as steel, brass, iron, bronze, or copper. Although lead bullets can't puncture the bulletproof vests worn by police officers, these cop-killer bullets can.

In 1989, Patrick Purdy opened fire on a Stockton, California, elementary school playground with an assault rifle. This shooting spree ended with five children murdered and twenty-nine others wounded. Shocked Americans, particularly parents, were increasingly upset by instances of gun violence on school grounds. Purdy's attack had been the fifth instance of a school shooting in one year. Following this tragic shooting, several states passed laws banning semiautomatic assault weapons. And in 1994, Congress did the same when it passed the Violent Crime Control and Law Enforcement Act. This law banned both the manufacture and ownership of semi-automatic rifles, handguns or shotguns (although exceptions were made for a few semiautomatic rifles used by hunters).

At the same time, gun culture and gun violence wasn't only invading the nation's schools. It was also becoming a big problem in private homes across America. As families splintered and an increasingly fast-paced life increased emotional stress on family members, incidents of domestic violence seemed to increase. And more and more, violence between a husband and his wife, a girlfriend and her boyfriend, or a parent and his or her kids came to a fatal head due to the presence of a gun in the home.

A FAMILY TORN APART: THE MENENDEZ BROTHERS CASE

One of the most talked about and shocking examples of a family torn apart by guns was the 1989 Menendez murders. On the evening of August 20, 1989, Jose and Kitty Menendez were lounging in the family room of their $4 million, twenty-three-room mansion in Beverly Hills watching a James Bond movie called *The Spy Who Loved Me*. The couple's two sons, twenty-one-year-old Lyle and eighteen-year-old Erik, had gone out.

At around 10 PM, a car drove up in front of the Menendez mansion and two men got out. Although the house—formerly rented by the likes of Prince and Elton John—boasted a high-tech security system, the two men succeeded in entering. They moved stealthily into the family room where Jose and Kitty were dozing in front of the television. Armed with shotguns, the killers shot off Jose's head. Alarmed, Kitty tried to escape, but she was gunned down, too. When the men realized that they were out of ammunition but that Kitty was still breathing, they loaded their guns with birdshot (small pellets) and killed her. They didn't want her to identify them to the police.

Later, when the police arrived, they found the couple dead, surrounded by pools of blood. Even though the killers tried not to leave any evidence, the identity of the two men was soon discovered: Jose and Kitty's two sons, Lyle and Erik. Only a few weeks before, the two handsome brothers had been watching a program on television called the *Billionaire Boys Club*. This show was based on a real group of young men from Beverly Hills who murdered the father of one of the group's members. Watching the movie, Lyle and Erik decided to kill their own father. He was too strict and hard to please and was planning to disinherit them in his will. They decided they would have to kill their mother as well since she was so emotionally dependent on their father. After long court proceedings that kept the nation riveted to the nightly news, in 1996 Lyle and Erik were finally sentenced to life imprisonment without parole for the shotgun slayings of their parents.

One result of growing public concern over cases of domestic violence was a 1996 federal law that made it illegal for anyone convicted of domestic violence to keep either guns or ammunition. Other more recent laws have followed the growing number of school shootings. In the weeks that followed the Columbine High School massacre, for example, the Senate passed a flurry of gun-control legislation, which included a call for private sellers at gun shows to run background checks on buyers and a requirement that all handguns be sold with trigger locks. Currently, both houses are studying many bills, including:

- The Firearms Safety and Consumer Protection Act, a bill that would expand the powers of the secretary of the treasury to regulate the manufacture, distribution, and sale of firearms and ammunition
- The Child Handgun Injury Prevention Act, a bill that would regulate the design, manufacture,

performance of, and sale of handguns in order to prevent children from unintentionally shooting themselves

- The Gun Show Accountability Act, a bill that would monitor the sale of firearms at gun shows
- The Internet Gun Trafficking Act, a bill that would regulate the sale of guns over the Internet

Guns at the State and Local Level

Up until now, we have looked at the major gun control laws passed by the federal government—laws shaped by the authority of the Constitution. However, throughout the twentieth century, not only the federal government but state and even some city, or municipal, governments have passed important laws concerning gun ownership, possession, and use. After all, under the Constitution, each state was allowed to have its own militia of private citizens that could bear arms. And it fell to each state to regulate these militias and how, when, and where its citizens could use arms. This wasn't up to the federal government.

One of the Anti-Federalists fears was of a federal government that was armed and powerful while the people were unarmed and weak. As a result, although the federal government could pass laws that affected gun use and ownership (taxing the sale of arms; enforcing the civil rights of all citizens, which indirectly meant all citizens shared the right to bear arms; regulating trade between the states, which allowed Congress to restrict gun sales from one state to another), states could, and did, pass laws that dealt directly with the right to bear arms within their borders.

The great majority of gun control laws are state and municipal laws. Just as the federal government turns to the U.S. Constitution when making federal laws, each state has its own constitution which governs the laws it can make. Since constitutions vary from state to state, so do the attitudes about guns and the type of gun laws that can be passed.

State Laws

Each state has its own laws concerning guns. Since the people who make laws are elected every four years, lawmakers change. This means that laws change, too. If you want to be absolutely up-to-date on exactly what the gun laws are in your state or city, you should check with your local police department. Most gun laws deal with the following gun-related issues:

- **Gun ID**—A few states require gun owners to carry owner identification cards that allow police to trace a weapon to its owner.

Colton Joshua Tooley opened fire with an AK-47 rifle on the University of Texas campus in Austin on September 28, 2010, leaving many critics to question why such powerful firearms are legal.

- **Carrying Guns in Plain View**—In some states it is legal for a person to carry a gun out in the open.

- **Carrying a Concealed Weapon**—The opposite of carrying a gun in plain view is concealing it from view. Many states allow all citizens to carry concealed guns. Others give the right only to certain professionals, such as police detectives or security guards. Still others prohibit concealed weapons altogether.

- **Gun Registration**—Some states require all guns to be registered. Large cities such as New York and Chicago, which have some of the strictest gun control laws in the country, also require registration.

- **Gun Purchase Permits**—In some states, you have to get a license before you can even buy either a handgun or a rifle.

- **Waiting Periods**—Quite a few states require a waiting period before you can buy a gun. The waiting period allows police to do a background check and to make sure that you are old enough to own a gun and that you have no criminal record. Any problem means no gun.

- **Keeping Guns Away from Kids**—Many parents keep guns in the home. Many kids find them and play with them. Many guns accidentally go off, wounding or killing whoever happens to be in the way. Such accidents have led several states to require that parents store guns in safe places if there is a chance of kids being around or that parents put trigger locks or safety locks on their guns.

- **Guns on School Property**—Remember the story told earlier about Patrick Purdy opening fire on a school playground in Stockton, California? Well, this is only one of many such stories. And then there are the thousands of kids who confess to bringing guns to school every day. To help avoid dangerous situations, several states have passed laws prohibiting people from carrying guns on school property or onto school buses. In the meantime, more and more schools are setting up metal detectors to stop students from bringing guns into schools.

- **Gun Disqualification**—Every state disqualifies certain people from owning guns. Such people include criminals, minors, drug addicts, or people with certain mental illnesses. It is felt that guns would be extra dangerous in such people's hands.

Gun Laws at the Municipal Level

In forty states, state gun laws cover everybody who lives in that particular state. However, in ten states, cities or municipalities are allowed to pass their own specific gun laws. This is especially common in very large cities where there is more crime. Cities like New York and Chicago have some of the toughest gun control laws in the country. New York law, for example, requires that anyone who buys a gun must get a permit. And once you have that gun, it must be registered. If you live in the boroughs of Manhattan or Brooklyn and you want a rifle, you'll have to supply four photos of yourself, be fingerprinted, and hand in two signed statements of good conduct.

Although many cities have passed laws banning guns, a couple have done just the opposite. In 1982, the small town of Kennesaw, Georgia, passed a law that obliged every head of household to keep a firearm as well as ammunition for it.

LAWYERS AND GUN MANUFACTURERS

Meanwhile, the most recent turn in American gun control is lawyers taking on gun manufacturers and dealers on behalf of cities and states upset with rising gun-related crimes. Perhaps you've heard about the many individuals and forty-six states who sued big tobacco manufacturers and won billions of dollars when it was proven that the cigarette companies knowingly sold life-threatening goods. In terms of guns, the same thing might just happen as private individuals and local communities attempt to get back some of the billions lost on gun-related violence each year.

To date, more than thirty cities (including Boston and Los Angeles) and counties have taken makers and sellers of guns to court, charging them with negligently distributing unsafe products. And in February 2000, a federal jury in Brooklyn found fifteen gun makers guilty of negligence in marketing and distributing their products. The municipalities say that firearms manufacturers resist low-cost trigger locks and other safety systems that could prevent so many tragic accidents at home. Furthermore, lack of control over sales and distribution allows some unscrupulous brokers to buy weapons in one state and sell them to gang members in another. And city lawyers say that the sheer size and efficiency of the profitable gun industry has become society's greatest enemy. This is because far more guns are made than are needed by law-abiding citizens. When the legal market can't absorb them, the guns go underground where they are easily bought and sold. It is said that manufacturers don't pay attention to who their dealers actually sell the guns to.

For their part, gun manufacturers and dealers say that the problem is the state and federal governments. It is the government who should be making more laws and who should be enforcing them. In response to these new charges, gun control opponents have pushed at least forty-four state governments to consider passing laws that will protect the gun industry from local and even individual lawsuits.

THE COURTS

While the legislative branch is responsible for making laws and the executive branch is responsible for carrying them out, the judicial branch must make sure that these laws are legal. Making sure that they are legal means making sure that these laws don't conflict with the law of the land contained in the Constitution.

The judicial branch of the federal government consists of the federal courts. These are courts that hear cases that come to them because somebody or some group believes that a certain new law or legal ruling is unconstitutional. After hearing a case, the court checks with the Constitution. Is this new law or ruling in accordance with the words set down by the Founding

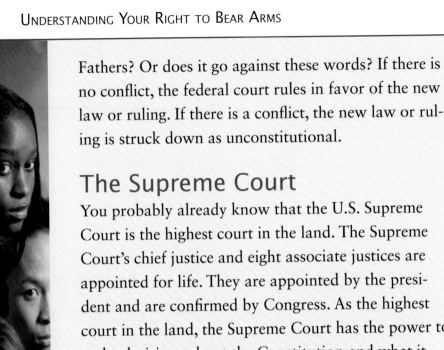

Fathers? Or does it go against these words? If there is no conflict, the federal court rules in favor of the new law or ruling. If there is a conflict, the new law or ruling is struck down as unconstitutional.

The Supreme Court

You probably already know that the U.S. Supreme Court is the highest court in the land. The Supreme Court's chief justice and eight associate justices are appointed for life. They are appointed by the president and are confirmed by Congress. As the highest court in the land, the Supreme Court has the power to make decisions about the Constitution and what it means. It can also declare a law unconstitutional.

When the Court does decide to hear one of the many cases that have been presented to it, it judges whether or not an issue is constitutional not only by examining and interpreting the words of the Constitution, but by looking at how past courts ruled on similar issues. This is called looking at precedent (precedent refers to a prior decision). Although the Court might decide to overturn an earlier court's ruling, in general it uses precedent as a guide. When a decision is finally made, however, not all nine judges have to be in agreement. If all are, then the decision is unanimous. Frequently, a decision has a majority opinion (that of the greater number of judges whose decision is law) and a minority or dissenting opinion

In a country that was founded on the will of its citizens to stand up against an oppressive government, but which today sees horrific gun violence, the debate over the right to bear arms will likely go on for years to come in the United States.

(that of the one or several judges who disagree with the majority).

Because the Supreme Court is interested in the "constitutionality" of a certain issue or law, it often judges an issue or law from a different viewpoint than that of lawmakers, government officials, special interest groups, or common citizens like you and me. Throughout the history of the United States, the twenty-seven words of the Second Amendment have been interpreted in many different ways. These interpretations have depended on many factors, such as the people doing the interpreting, where they live or lived, and at what point in time they were living.

A twenty-six-year-old man living in a crime-ridden neighborhood of Washington, D.C., in the twenty-first century will have a very different opinion about the right to bear arms than an eighty-four-year-old woman living on a farm in rural Kentucky in the 1880s or a wealthy married couple in their thirties living in a Manhattan penthouse in the 1950s. Today especially, America is becoming an increasingly diverse place. It is only natural that so many different people would have different opinions about what the Founding Fathers meant by those twenty-seven words, and what those words mean in today's America.

However, while parents and politicians, lawyers and law students, those who support gun control and those against it have spent much of the last two centuries (but especially the twentieth century) debating what "the right to bear and keep arms" exactly means, the Supreme Court has rarely heard cases dealing with this controversial amendment. In fact, since the Bill of Rights came into being in 1791, the Court has heard few cases that relate to the Second Amendment. One recent case was *McDonald v. Chicago,* on June 28, 2010.

Some State Court Decisions

Forty-three out of fifty American states have constitutions that protect the right to bear arms. Just as the Supreme Court bases its rulings on the words of the U.S. Constitution, the state courts base theirs on the text of their own constitutions, most of which have clauses similar to the Second Amendment.

Early on, state courts seemed hesitant to place limits on their citizens' right to bear arms. Kentucky was the first state to take the plunge. The year was 1813 and the state's law prohibiting its citizens from carrying concealed weapons was the first of its kind in America. Kentucky was also the first state to make a court decision on the right to bear arms. In 1822, in the case of *Bliss v. Commonwealth,* the court heard the appeal of a man who had been convicted of walking around town with a sword concealed in his cane.

The charges were dropped when the court decided that the right to bear arms meant bearing all arms, not just those carried in plain view. The court's decision was based on the Kentucky Constitution's statement that "the right of citizens to bear arms in defense of themselves and the State must be preserved."

A similar case occurred some years later in Georgia. In 1837, the state had passed a law banning the sale of most pistols. In 1846, the Georgia Supreme Court overturned this law. It found the law unconstitutional and based its argument on the second clause of the Second Amendment which it interpreted as "the right of the whole people, old and young, men, women and boys, and not militia only, to keep and bear arms of every description, and not such merely as are used by the militia, shall not be infringed, curtailed, or broken in upon, in the smallest degree."

These early decisions are of interest because they declared that an individual citizen's right to bear arms was absolute. As the nineteenth century wore on, society would change and so would gun culture. Reflecting these changes would be the attitude of the courts, which began to uphold restrictions on ownership and possession of arms.

As early as the 1840s, state courts began to support weapon control laws. In 1840, in *Aymette v. State*, the Supreme Court of Tennessee based its support of a state gun control law on the state constitution, which declared "that the citizens of this State have a right to keep and to bear arms for their common defense; but the Legislature shall have power, by law, to regulate the wearing of arms with a view to prevent crime." Other state courts made similar decisions based on similar clauses in their constitutions. The result was that while courts supported citizens' keeping arms, they felt that the states had the right to step in and regulate their use in order to ensure public peace and safety.

This view—that the right to keep and bear arms can be restricted, or even prohibited, by the government—has continued to dominate thousands of state and local court decisions throughout the twentieth century as well. At the same time however, some courts have also ruled that the right to keep and bear arms means that individual citizens do have a right to keep weapons such as handguns and revolvers for purposes of self-defense. The supreme courts of Montana, Colorado, and Oregon all based such decisions on their own state constitutions.

In a 1980 case, for example, the Supreme Court of Oregon explained its ruling in the following manner: "We are not unmindful that there is current controversy over the wisdom of the right to bear arms, and that the original motivations for such a provision might not seem compelling if debated as a new issue. Our task, however...is to respect the principles given the status of constitutional guarantees and limitations by the drafters; it is not to abandon these principles when this fits the needs of the moment."

The court must have realized that its decision to let individuals bear arms for self-defense would be opposed by supporters of gun control. However, it based its decision on its state constitution, which said, "the people shall have the right to bear arms for the defense of themselves, and the State."

Preamble to the Constitution

We the People of the United States, in order to form a more perfect Union, establish Justice, insure domestic Tranquility, provide for the common defense, promote the general Welfare, and secure the Blessings of Liberty to ourselves and our Posterity, do ordain and establish this Constitution for the United States of America.

On September 25, 1789, Congress transmitted to the state legislatures twelve proposed amendments, two of which, having to do with congressional representation and congressional pay, were not adopted. The remaining ten amendments became the Bill of Rights.

The Bill of Rights

Amendment I

Congress shall make no law respecting an establishment of religion, or prohibiting the free exercise thereof; or abridging the freedom of speech, or of the press; or the right of the people peaceably to assemble, and to petition the Government for a redress of grievances.

Amendment II

A well regulated Militia, being necessary to the security of a free State, the right of the people to keep and bear Arms, shall not be infringed.

Amendment III

No Soldier shall, in time of peace be quartered in any house, without the consent of the Owner, nor in time of war, but in a manner to be prescribed by law.

Amendment IV

The right of the people to be secure in their persons, houses, papers, and effects, against unreasonable searches and seizures, shall not be violated, and no Warrants shall issue, but upon probable cause, supported by Oath or affirmation, and particularly describing the place to be searched, and the persons or things to be seized.

Amendment V

No person shall be held to answer for a capital, or otherwise infamous crime, unless on a presentment or indictment of a Grand Jury, except in cases arising in the land or naval forces, or in the Militia, when in actual service in time of War or public danger; nor shall any person be subject for the same offence to be twice put in jeopardy of life or limb; nor shall be compelled in any criminal case to be a witness against himself, nor be deprived of life, liberty, or property, without due process of law; nor shall private property be taken for public use, without just compensation.

Amendment VI

In all criminal prosecutions, the accused shall enjoy the right to a speedy and public trial, by an impartial jury of the State and district wherein the crime shall have been committed, which district shall have been previously ascertained by law, and to be informed of the nature and cause of the accusation; to be confronted with the witnesses against him; to have compulsory process for obtaining witnesses in his favor, and to have the Assistance of Counsel for his defense.

Amendment VII

In Suits at common law, where the value in controversy shall exceed twenty dollars, the right of trial by jury shall be preserved, and no fact tried by a jury, shall be otherwise reexamined in any Court of the United States, than according to the rules of the common law.

Amendment VIII

Excessive bail shall not be required, nor excessive fines imposed, nor cruel and unusual punishments inflicted.

Amendment IX

The enumeration in the Constitution, of certain rights, shall not be construed to deny or disparage others retained by the people.

Amendment X

The powers not delegated to the United States by the Constitution, nor prohibited by it to the States, are reserved to the States respectively, or to the people.

amendment An addition, change, or refinement to the U.S. Constitution.

appeal When the ruling of a lower court is challenged and the case is then heard by a higher court.

Athenian A resident of Athens.

automatic rifle A shoulder firearm that fires one bullet after another when the trigger is pulled and held; also referred to as a machine gun.

ban To prohibit.

bayonet A daggerlike piece of steel placed on the muzzle of a gun allowing a soldier to finish off the enemy by stabbing.

Brady Act The Brady Handgun Violence Prevention Act requires federal background checks on anyone attempting to purchase a firearm in the United States.

citizen A person who is legally recognized as a member of a particular geographic territory.

Civil Rights Act The Civil Rights Act of 1866 allowed anyone born in the United States except Native Americans the right to full U.S. citizenship.

civil war A war between two groups within the same country. The American Civil War was fought from 1861 to 1865 between the slave states in the South (the Confederacy) and the free states in the North (the Union).

Constitution The supreme legal document of the United States, which was initiated in 1789 and has

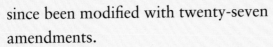

since been modified with twenty-seven amendments.

constitutional Something that is in accordance with the U.S. Constitution.

convicted The state of being guilty of a criminal offense as judged by a court of law.

federal Of or relating to the federal government.

felony A crime categorized among the most serious, such as murder, rape, or robbery.

Founding Fathers The group of politicians that adopted the U.S. Constitution in 1787.

gun control Laws that restrict how or whether a person may buy, sell, or own a gun; legal and social efforts to regulate the distribution and use of firearms.

handgun A small handheld firearm such as a pistol or revolver.

House of Representatives The lower house of the U.S. Congress.

Lakota The American Indian people of western South Dakota.

legislation Laws that are enacted by a legislative body.

militia An army of private citizens that is called upon in times of emergency.

musket A long firearm, worn slung over the shoulder, that was an ancestor of the rifle.

opponent Someone who disagrees with and fights against a movement or idea.

Parliament The British governmental organization consisting of the sovereign, the House of Lords, and the House of Commons.

ratification Approval of a measure, law, or amendment.

Revolutionary War The American war fought between 1775 and 1783 that sought to free thirteen former British colonies in North America from the rule of England.

rifle A shoulder gun in which spiral grooves cut inside the barrel put a spin on shot bullets, making them more accurate.

Saturday night special A cheap, poorly made handgun.

waiting period A short period of time between applying to buy a gun and actually getting one, during which police can check the buyer's background.

Brady Campaign to Prevent Gun Violence (BCPGV)

1225 Eye Street NW, Suite 1100

Washington, DC 20005

(202) 898-0792

Web site: http://www.bradycampaign.org

The BCPGV is devoted to creating an America free of gun violence.

Bureau of Alcohol, Tobacco, Firearms and Explosives (ATF)

Office of Public and Governmental Affairs

99 New York Avenue NE, Room 5S 144

Washington, DC 20226

Web site: http://www.atf.gov

A branch of the U.S. Department of Justice, the ATF protects communities from illegal activities such as violent crime, terrorism, and illegal firearms.

Citizens Committee for the Right to Keep and Bear Arms (CCRKBA)

Liberty Park

12500 N.E. Tenth Place

Bellevue, WA 98005

(800) 486-6963

Web site: http://www.ccrkba.org

Founded in 1971, the CCRKBA is a gun rights organization with 615,000 members.

Coalition to Stop Gun Violence (CSGV)

1424 L Street NW, Suite 2-1

Washington, DC 20005

(202) 408-0061

Web site: http://www.csgv.org

The Coalition to Stop Gun Violence seeks to secure freedom from gun violence through research, strategic engagement and effective policy advocacy.

Federal Bureau of Investigation (FBI)

FBI Headquarters

935 Pennsylvania Avenue NW

Washington, DC 20535-0001

(202) 324-3000

Web site: http://www.fbi.gov

The FBI is the law enforcement agency of the U.S. government that conducts both criminal investigation and intelligence gathering.

Liberty Belles

P.O. Box 3631

Salem, OR 97302

Web site: http://www.libertybelles.org

Liberty Belles is a grassroots, freedom-focused organization inside and out, working to inform its members and the public of their right to keep and bear arms

National Rifle Association (NRA)

11250 Waples Mill Road, Suite 1

Fairfax, VA 22030

(703) 267-1000

Web site: http://www.nra.org

Established in 1871, the NRA is a nonprofit organization dedicated to protecting the Second Amendment.

Second Amendment Foundation (SAF)
James Madison Building
12500 N.E. Tenth Place
Bellevue, WA 98005
(800) 426-4302
Web site: http://www.saf.org
The Second Amendment Foundation is dedicated to promoting a
better understanding of the Second Amendment and informing
the public about the gun control debate.

WEB SITES

Due to the changing nature of Internet links, Rosen
Publishing has developed an online list of Web sites
related to the subject of this book. This site is updated
regularly. Please use this link to access the list:

http://www.rosenlinks.com/pfcd/arms

Amar, Akhil Reed. *America's Constitution: A Biography*. New York, NY: Random House, 2006.

Beeman, Richard. *Plain, Honest Men: The Making of the American Constitution*. New York, NY: Random House, 2010.

Burbick, Joan. *Gun Show Nation: Gun Culture and American Democracy*. New York, NY: New Press, 2007.

Canada, Geoffrey. *Fist Stick Knife Gun: A Personal History of Violence*. Boston, MA: Beacon Press, 2010.

Churchill, Robert H. *To Shake Their Guns in the Tyrant's Face: Libertarian Political Violence and the Origins of the Militia Movement*. Ann Arbor, MI: University of Michigan Press, 2009.

Collier, Paul. *Wars, Guns, and Votes: Democracy in Dangerous Places*. New York, NY: Harper Perennial, 2010.

Cornell, Saul. *A Well-Regulated Militia: The Founding Fathers and the Origins of Gun Control in America*. New York, NY: Oxford University Press, 2008.

Doherty, Brian. *Gun Control on Trial: Inside the Supreme Court Battle Over the Second Amendment*. Washington, DC: Cato Institute, 2009.

Feldman, Richard. *Ricochet: Confessions of a Gun Lobbyist*. Hoboken, NJ: Wiley, 2007.

Halbrook, Stephen P. *The Founders' Second Amendment: Origins of the Right to Bear Arms*. Landham, MD: Ivan R. Dee, 2008.

Henigan, Dennis A. *Lethal Logic: Exploding the Myths That Paralyze American Gun Policy*. Dulles, VA: Potomac Books, 2009.

Jacobs, James B. *Can Gun Control Work?* (Studies in Crime and Public Policy). New York, NY: Oxford University Press, 2004.

LaPierre, Wayne. *The Global War on Your Guns: Inside the U.N. Plan to Destroy the Bill of Rights*. Nashville, TN: Thomas Nelson, 2006.

Lott, John R. *The Bias Against Guns: Why Almost Everything You've Heard About Gun Control Is Wrong*. Washington, DC: Regnery Press, 2003.

Roleff, Tamara. *Gun Control* (Opposing Viewpoints). New York, NY: Greenhaven, 2007.

Spitzer, Robert J. *Gun Control: A Documentary and Reference Guide* (Documentary and Reference Guides). New York, NY: Greenwood, 2009.

Stewart, David O. *The Summer of 1787: The Men Who Invented the Constitution* (The Simon & Schuster America Collection). New York, NY: Simon & Schuster, 2008.

Van Wyk, Charl. *Shooting Back: The Right and Duty of Self-Defense*. Washington, DC: WND Books, 2007.

Wilson, Harry L. *Guns, Gun Control, and Elections: The Politics and Policy of Firearms*. Lanham, MD: Rowman & Littlefield Publishers, 2006.

ABOUT THE AUTHORS

Nathaniel Cross is a writer living in New Jersey.

Michael A. Sommers is a writer who frequently contributes to the *New York Times*, the *Globe and Mail*, and the *International Herald Tribune*.

PHOTO CREDITS